Greener Pastures

by
Florence Virginia Wilkins Coleman

Angelee Coleman Grider, Editor

M.O.R.E. Publishers Corp.
St. Louis, MO

Greener Pastures

by
Florence Virginia Wilkins Coleman

M.O.R.E. Publishers Corp.
St. Louis, Missouri
Email: MOREPublishersCO@AOL.com

Angelee Coleman Grider, editor

ISBN: 978-0-9801647-2-5

Library of Congress Control Number: 2007909443

Printed in the United States of America

A Look Inside...

Florence's Moment

Della, Diane, Florence

This is the moment when I get to finish going through stuff and the moment when it will all be put together to complete my book publishing.

I hope you enjoy what you find. Whatever my daughter didn't throw away, it's in here. If you find any more sayings, write your very own book.

About the Author
(As of July 15, 1946)

(Excerpts from an application survey, Rust College, Holly Springs, Mississippi)

Born: January 20, 1923

Home Address: Collierville, Tennessee

County: Marshall

State: Mississippi

Church Membership: C.M.E.

Parents: Aaron Wilkins I (Father)
                Ora Moody Wilkins (Mother)

Parents' Occupation: farmers

Personal Health: "Not so good."

High School: Mississippi Industrial College (M.I. College) 1941 – 1945

Principal: Miss M.E. Shannon

Purpose

<u>Greener Pastures</u> is a collection of family and community literary gatherings. The book includes original works by me along with historical pieces that I saved and wanted to share to contribute to the historical relevance of life here on earth. Hopefully an understanding of mankind will be learned from reading the pieces.

Preface

Keep in mind that sayings in the book are not necessarily quoted from any particular person. Some have been gathered from newspaper clippings, others from what was actually heard by the author.

Some material was impossible to give credit to anyone because none was listed. However, it was a bit of history the author thought would be of some essence to the readers.

THE EDITOR

Dedication

I dedicate this bit of history quips to my family.
"Carry on the tradition of leaving a legacy."
Write Black Woman Write! Sing Black Man Sing!

A Family Reunion Celebration, 1984
at
Old Mt. Pisgah C.M.E. Church
Cayce, Mississippi

Row 1: 1) unknown (UK), 2) unknown, 3) Marie's baby, (seated in chairs),
4) Lucille Washington Cuff, 5) Willie Ruth Wilkins, 6) Ora Moody Wilkins
with baby, 7) Edna Hall, 8) Johnnie Wilkins, 9) Florence Virginia Wilkins
Coleman, 10) Charlene Wilkins, 10) UK, 11) UK, 12) Kim Wilkins

Row 2: 1) Isaiah Garrison, 2) Sheila Wilkins, 3) Marie Wilkins, 4) Joseph
Hines (purple cap), 5) Count Lebby [child with Mom], 6) Fannie Belle
Wilkins Lebby (large hat), 7) Herman Wilkins, 6) Aaron Wilkins Jr. II,
7) Earye Bridgeforth Wilkins, 8)Nina Mae Hale Wilkins (glasses), 9)UK,
10)UK, 11) Tina, 12) Ada Wilkins

Row 3: 1) UK, 2) UK, 3) UK, 4) UK, 5) Christopher Earl Grider, 6) UK,
7) UK (pink shirt), 8) Joseph Hines (hat), 10) Patty Wilkins (black blouse),
11) UK (pink flower blouse), 12) Edwin Marcellus T. Grider (red hat, white
shorts), 13) Lloyd Benjamin Wilkins, 14) Aaron Wilkins Jr. III (right, hat)

Row 4: Church steps – 1) Cleotra Smith, 2) Rev. George W. Coleman Jr.,
3) Brenda Wilkins, 4) Vel Virginia Lee Wilkins Barrino (red shirt),
4) Natasha Garrison (blue blouse)

Steps, 2nd row: 1) UK, 2)UK

Steps, 3rd Row: 1) Dorothy Ann Garrison, 2) Angelee Coleman Grider,
3) Mary Jean Wilkins Wells, 4) Corrine Hines, (5) Jimmie Hines

5

FAMOUS WILL

Date: Wednesday – June 5, 1946

If things are like I see them, that is, if I can see straight in my mind, and the way things will come out to be, I will make my Last Will and Testimony.

I, Florence Virginia Wilkins; being sound of mind (I hope) this – bright Wednesday morning June 5th, in the Year of Our Lord (One Thousand-Nine Hundred and Forty-Six) – Do hereby state and make my will as follows:

Item to Mother: I leave my diploma, coat, and chair so that she may rock away her worries when I am gone.

Item to Father: I leave my trunk and key so that he may lock up all of his secret treasure.

Item to Sister Mary: I leave all of my jewelry to always remember me.

Item to Sister Della: I leave my suite of furniture to always remember May 23rd, 1945.

Item to Brother Aaron Jr.: I leave my class ring to recall (back) memories.

Item to Brother Jemes: I leave my picture, comb, glass, and my bank so he may be able to buy him a tuxedo and keep his hair well groomed.

Item to my middle brother Cleaveland: I leave my Ever-sharp pen, table, and my artist work.

Item to Brother Hermon: I leave my Bell Bottom trousers and my boots. Bear in mind how I would talk about the boots.

Item to my Nephew L.B. Jones Wilkins: I leave all my chickens and what so ever he wants to keep that will make him happy.

Item to my Nephew A.D. and Alton Jr. Kizer: I leave to A.D. my white pants that he may have cut drapes to be in style. To Alton Jr., I leave all of my caps and the same opportunity that L.B. has.

Item to my Niece Jannie Florence Kizer: I leave all of my nice dresses, the addresses of all of my formal boy friends, so that when she becomes in her teen years she will keep up the good work of her old Aunte, so that her aunt's memories will still live on in the Popularity World.

Item to my friends and relatives: I will that you all will look into the Future and not the Past, yet always look back along the road where you once came and whatever you see fit that you want in your possession of mine, as a token, it is yours for the asking.

As for me, it's just "So Long", "Been nice knowing you all these few years", "Did appreciate everything each of you did for me, whether good or bad". Bye, it's better this way.

(Signed)
Florence Virginia Wilkins (Coleman)

A Dedication of Sorts– An Essay

Called By Name and Nailed To The Cross

During our pastor's recognition service, I had asked the congregation to "Please stand and let us read together Jeremiah 1:5." They did, but it took them so long to find the scripture. Then we finally began reading.

> I knew you before you were formed within your mother's womb; before you were born I sanctified you and appointed you as my spokesman to the world.
>
> Jeremiah 1:5

After I asked them to "Please be seated", I continued with my contribution to the program. This was my dedication to my pastor, Rev. Hubie L. Nelson. I continued.

As with Jeremiah, the Lord said to Rev. Hubie L. Nelson, "I knew you before you were formed within your mother's womb; before you were born I sanctified you and appointed you as my spokesman to the world."

However, then in the New Testament Jesus speaks that the "Son of Man" must suffer many things:

Now as you read, you must have noticed that these two (2) commands are not alike. They are different.

Yet both say something about Rev. Hubie L. Nelson.

First the references say that Rev. Hubie L. Nelson was no stranger to God from the time of the world's creation.

When Rev. Hubie Nelson was conceived, God appointed him to be a spokesman to the world.

How was Rev. Nelson to do that?

He was to do it in season and out of season.

He was to speak from the top of Mt. Zion to the crown of Mt. Pisgah.

He was to stay bound by the commands in sickness and in health until death do him part from the bridegroom Jesus Christ and from the Church.

Has he done what he was called to do?

Yes. So let the church say, Amen.

Now if he says by your witness that he was set aside, called, and sent as a spokesman, why has he been nailed to the cross?

Then you may want to know, when was he nailed to the cross as between two thieves?

First, Rev. Hubie Nelson was nailed to the cross when Jesus' blood ran down and Rev. Hubie Nelson's sins were taken from him, and laid on the shoulders of Jesus Christ.

Secondly, when was he nailed to the cross?

He was destined to the cross when his mother's womb opened and granted us the one to shoulder the burdens of this earth.

Remember that when you take up Christ's causes you by silence are agreeing to bear the cross.

Third, we nailed him to the cross.

When?

We nailed him to the cross when we did not see the insight that he said that he had been given from God.

We nailed him to the cross when we did not obey God's words as delivered through him, Rev. Nelson as the pastor.

So I ask today, if he was anointed, and called by name, why was he nailed to the cross?

"A Final Word"

Dedicated to me, myself, and I (after the marriage of my daughter)

Growing up also means growing away. A wise parent recognizes that a youngster must first of all fall out of love with his parents before he can fall in love with another person and begin a new family – new life cycle. Gibran phrased the principle here beautifully in The Prophet:

"Your children are not your children. They are the sons and daughters of life's longing for itself. They come through you but not from you, and though they are with you, yet they belong not to you.

You may give them your love but not your thoughts, for they have their own thoughts. You may strive to be like them, but seek not to make them like you.

For life goes not backward, nor tarries with yesterday."

The wisest parents ask only that a child grow into a decent human being, actualized in his own way. When this goal is reached, then a child will love and respect his parents because it is a natural outgrowth of genuine feeling and not because he is indebted to them.

There are many ways for helping a child to grow up. If we remember nothing else, let us keep in mind that to bring up a child in the way he should go, we have to travel that way ourselves once in a while.

13

Famous Speeches
For All Occasions

"Everyday is Harvest Day" or "Harvest Day is Coming"

Before we can talk about Harvest, we must first speak about agriculture, and agriculture is the growing of crop and the raising of animals in order to satisfy man's needs.

This includes farming, dairying, ranching, poultry raising, fruit growing, and many other things. Through agriculture man provides himself with nearly all his food and clothing. Agriculture has shaped the growth of civilization and plays a vital role in improving the well-being and health of individuals. After laboring for many days in various ways of agriculture man looks forward to the day of harvesting, when he will gather in the results of his labor from the sweat of his brow.

In St. Matthews, the 20th Chapter, and verse 7A, Christ said "Go ye also into the vineyard and what so ever is right, that shall ye receive."

We too are laborers in God's vineyard. He is the master. We are the workers. Let us toil on through the storm and rain so when he calls for us to bring in the results from our labouring, we too can say as the songwriter put it, "So let us work on for Harvest Day is coming."

A Church Welcome

(Author Unknown)

Adapted, revised version by the editor

To the mistress or master of ceremony, pastor, pulpit guests, members, friends, visitors, and all of you my Father God's children:

It is indeed a pleasure and grand opportunity to extend to you a welcome from the depths of my heart. I do not have words at my command that will enable me to offer to you the welcome that my heart is dictating.

We are so glad to have you with us. Your presence assures us of your receptive feelings. Your participation will peak your interest, and this church, the pastor, and our friends will appreciate your endeavors.

History tells us that God opened the doors of all churches more than 19 Hundred years ago through His son Jesus Christ, who hung, bled, and died on the cross that we might have a right to the eternal, everlasting tree of life.

The doors of the church are still open and God is still saying, "Whosoever will, let him come". Therefore, we say to you, come. You are welcome, welcome, welcome.

A Welcome From My Church

To the pastor, pulpit guests, members of Mt. Pisgah, the most distinct guests, visitors and friends;

I count this one of the greatest moments of my life as well as the privilege to come in your presence to extend to you a few words of welcome.

Welcome means to receive with gladness and hospitality. Just what are we trying to do? We are trying to receive both mothers and fathers with gladness. Knowing that today is mother's day, and that you are guests, we want you to feel welcome here. We want you to feel just as welcome as if you were at home.

Please always remember that these doors swing from the hinges of welcome and the pillars of this building rest upon the pillars of welcome.

We want you to feel just as welcome here as Jesus Christ felt when He went riding into Jerusalem, and as some went before him saying, "Hosanna, Blessed is He that cometh in the name of the Lord." I feel that deep down in their hearts there was a little, small voice saying, "Welcome, welcome, welcome."

An Invitation

To the Master of Ceremony, Pastor, pulpit guest, members of Hearn Grove, visitors, and friends.

First, I must say the subject is "Reaching the Verdict" and the word verdict may be defined as a decision reached by anyone.

The next question comes to mind refers to us, as young people trying to make a decision in many ways during this social unrest.

Since this is such a broad subject, I shall limit mine to Christianity standpoints. We must reach a verdict to attend Sunday school and church every Sunday and be a part of the service.

Paul reached the verdict when he said, (and I quote) "I am crucified with Christ yet I live, but not I but Christ Jesus in me".

That means for one who has made a decision and dedicated his life to Christ, the vanity of this world is "crucified with Christ", but I live not able physically to withstand the wiles of the devil. Yet all things are possible for me to do, with Christ in me, to strengthen me.

The words of the preacher in the Chapter 12 book of Ecclesiastes says, "Remember now thou Creator in the days of thou youth." This is the time to reach the verdict. Thank you.

A Look at a Town's History

A bit history that I found about Holly Springs, Mississippi
where I attended school

1) Holly Springs is a town in northern Mississippi near the Tennessee line. It is a pretty, fresh, wholesome place built on high grounds, set among hills that are overrun with flowers in the rich soil and antebellum homes.

2) The railway boom was in 1860. The Mississippi Central train ran from Canton to Holly Springs.

3) In 1851, Joseph Holt Ingram, a New Englander founded a parish at Okolona, Mississippi and operated a boys' school at Holly Springs' St. Thomas Hall.

4) During the late seventies the C.M.E. Church (north) established a Negro college at Holly Springs known as Shaw University. In 1890, the name was changed to Rust University.

5) In 1878, 1,400 of the 1,500 died of yellow fever in Holly Springs.

6) The leading writer of the Post War Era was Sherwood Bonner one of Holly Springs' greatest physician's daughter.

7) One of Holly Springs' senators was Edward C. Walthall a Confederate major General.

8) The Holly Springs Art Gallery was built in 1957, the home of the artist Kate Freeman Clark.

9) At least 96 years ago in Holly Springs, oil, and candles were used for lighting purposes.

10) All roads and streets were mud or sandy.

11) Schools and churches were framed buildings. Students had to walk 2 or 3 miles to the nearest school.

12) No ice was delivered publicly. Water wells were then considered necessity possessions.

13) The horses and buggies were merely luxury items. Even cotton wagons parked on the main streets.

14) Wood was used for fuel. Wooden benches were in front of stores for some customers.

15) Taxes were paid promptly.

16) No one received anything from the government, but a package of garden seeds.

17) No one had heard of pajamas.

18) Everyone had a front gate.

19) Every church had a revival, and an amen corner.

20) Doctors rode horsebacks, and there were more "coloreds" than white voters in the county.

A Look At A History of People

A. The renowned Mr. Rufus Thomas was a native of Cayce, Mississippi (March 26, 1917). No, his family was not always residents in Memphis, Tennessee. Mr. Thomas was a personality with WDIA-AM Radio in Memphis until his death in December 2001. He is most remembered for his songs and dances "Walking the Dog", "Do The Funky Chicken" and many others.

B. The graduating class of Tyson Elementary School had only 10 students, in the commencement exercises Wednesday, May 17, 1958; 2:00 P.M. at Nichols Chapel C.M.E. Church. The constituents were Shirley Ann Akens, Barbara Ruth Dockery, Cleo Dockery, Verline Ivy, Andrew Lee Jones, Helen Sharp, Ida B. Sharp, Epsie Tunstall, Ida Mae Young, and Willie Lee Wells.

C. In 1958, Achievement Day activities included such nice things as a morning session assembly with storytelling, spelling contests, a song festival, art displays, and an oratorical contest. The afternoon session involved athletic activities as the Potato Race, Sack Race, Broad Jump, Basketball games, and a Maypole Dance.

D. The Christian Methodist Episcopal Church (C.M.E.) operated a well-known college named Mississippi Industrial College, (M.I.) in 1905. The college was then located on

College Avenue, Highway 78, in Holly Springs, Mississippi.

E. The Young Men's Christian Association, better known as the YMCA, sponsored a state Federation of Hi-Y and Tri-Hi-Y Clubs. This information was on my son's membership card, in August, 1967

F. In 1968 Mississippi residents who lived near the State Line had a Tennessee address (Fact: my address was Route 2, Box 310; then later Box 323; both addresses were from Collierville, Tennessee 38017. I lived in Cayce, Mississippi. The system was changed in 2000. Yet amazingly according to an old letter from a friend of mine, in 1958, my address was Route 2, Box 173, Byhalia, Mississippi.

G. In March 1973 Mississippi Industrial College had thriving student clubs such as the Ministerial Alliance, the Student Improvement Program, a collegiate campus newspaper, a annual college yearbook, a drama society, a choir, a Cavalier Club which was a social club for young men, and a Social Science Club.

H. The State built a new high school for the blacks, 1st – 12th grade (about 1960). The name was Henry High School. Later the board of education changed it to a middle school, 1st – 8th grade (around 1972). An older building, previously predominated by whites, became the town's high school.

Then according to an April 19, 1989 news clipping, the Marshall County Board of Education delayed a plan to relocate students at the "white" Byhalia High School and Henry Jr. High. The predominately white PTA had requested that the children not be moved to the Henry Jr. High building. Grades 6, 7, and 8 were to go to Byhalia (the ragged building), and grades 9, 10, 11, and 12 were to go to Henry (the once new school). The PTA opposed a move even though according to the Superintendent Lawrence Autry who was Black, "recently constructed facilities at Henry, including a library, science lab and several classrooms, were intended for use by high school students". Did it take almost 30 years for someone to listen and to recognize that?

I.   In 1969, my daughter's freshman class (1968-69) was accused of starting a riot on Lane College's campus and burning the science building down. The school was closed indefinitely in March according to a Western Union Telegram that I received from the President.

J.   In 1979, the only thing you had to do to be a member of the Red Cross was to make a financial donation. Now you have to take tests.

K.   Damon Moore of Coldwater was the 23rd University of Mississippi student to receive a "Rhodes Scholarship" to study at Oxford University in England. (from a December 19, 1986 news clipping)

L.   Until 1989, at least two C.M.E. churches in the Northern Mississippi area continued to hold only one Sunday service each month. According to one of my notes that I found, I more information enlightened me. "I am 66" said Florence, "Now we will be having service every Sunday. Use to be only on the 2nd Sunday once a month. Then 2nd and 4th, twice a month. ...History was made tonight (August 30, 1989). First church conference after an Annual Conference." My church was one of those two churches to make a change.

M.   Thomas "The Hitman" Hearns who is well known as a World Middleweight Championship fighter is also a native of Mississippi. His mom married into our family. I liked her!

N.   Eddie Lee Smith Jr. joined the "March for Freedom" from Memphis (Tennessee) and Jackson, Mississippi during the Civil Rights movement in 1966. Smith, a teacher for 10 years in Marshall County, was the leader of the first march held in Holly Springs in 1964. He was also the first black Mayor of Holly Springs. Smith and his wife, Luberta worked in public relations before his death.

O.   S. T. Nero was the first president of the Marshall County branch of the NAACP.

P.   Marshall County Teachers Association had a 3-Article, 20 Sections, Preamble from which they were to be governed.

Q.   "A little pot's soon hot." A "pot" in 1958 was a cooking vessel.

Letter to Florence From M.I. College

Mississippi Industrial College
Holly Springs, Mississippi
January 25, 1961

Dear Senior:

I am happy to give you my advance congraulation (exact spelling) for your achievement this far along the educational ladder. In a few days you will be leaving the campus to go out and get a sip of your future life and try to impart some of the information and knowledge you have gained here at the Mississippi Industrial. It is my hope that your practice work will help to better acquaint you with your permanent life's occupation.

Below is an estimate of your graduation fees:

Cap, Gown and degree	$14.50
Thesis	$16.50
Class Pictures	$ 7.95
Class Dues	$15.00
Jewelry (ladies)	$24.95
(men)	$35.00
Invitations	$ .17 ½ each

Class pictures will not be made until March 11, 1961.

Sincerely yours
J. L. Watts, Sponsor

POETRY,
RHETORIC,
SONGS

Down To Earth Rhetoric
(authors unknown)

"Success is that place in a road where preparation and opportunity meet. But too few people recognize it, because too often it comes disguised as hard work." (Author unknown)

➢ **"High Resolve"**: I'll hold my candle high, and then perhaps I'll see the hearts of men above the sordidness of life, beyond misunderstandings and strife.

Though many deeds that others do seem foolish, rash and sinful too,

Just who am I to criticize?

What do I perceive with my dull eyes?

I'll hold my candle high, and then perhaps I'll see the hearts of men.

Author Unknown

➢ Walk into 1974 with a willing spirit, a clean heart, and sweet disposition.

➢ "Remember God's Blessing": Stop worrying about: (1) things you can't do anything about and (2) things that never happened.

Do You Believe...?

1984 – Cinders were used to "ease driving" during snowstorms. Just ask Joseph Johnson and Timothy Hines.

A country church raised $1,184.88 during one "Twelve Gates To The City" afternoon service.

One of Robert Altman's movie films, "Cookie's Fortune", includes locations of Holly Springs. Ask for a copy of the Pigeon Roost Newspaper, Volume 21, Number 10 (Wednesday). I forgot and cut the date off. They'll know what I'm talking about though. Just ask for it.

It only cost $2.00 to submit an application for admission to Mississippi Industrial College. Of course it was non-refundable.

You only had to enclose a money order of $1.00 made payable to the Mississippi State Board of Health in order to obtain a birth certificate, if you were born before November 1, 1912. (Information obtained from an application from the Division of Vital Statistics). On the application there is a question that reads: "If birth occurred before November 1, 1912, did you file a delayed birth certificate?"

Speaking of money orders, in April 1964, you could meet your mail carrier and purchase a money order for 20 cents, 30 cents, or 35 cents.

Schools in Mississippi always start in August or no later than the first week in September.

FOLKLORE POETRY

The Republicans' seedling sprouted and grew, in the simple minds of quite a few;

And these simple ones will vote alike,

As they cast their vote for dear old Ike;

As they go to the polls and vote for Ike.

Every since 1932 the Republicans' Party has been in a stew.

They have cussed the Democrats and called them bad names but the banks stayed open just the same.

When Hoover was in I lived on a farm.

A dollar bill looked long as your arm.

I never saw a ten-dollar bill, and if Ike gets back in I never will.

When Hoover was in things were mighty tight.

Rabbits were scared and fish wouldn't bite.

The men were too raggedy to go anywhere and women wore sacks for underwear.

So my friend, when there's voting to do,

Think back to 1932.

Would you rather live a life of ease?

Or have water, gravel, and black-eyed peas?

These Hoover days I'll never forget,
Every since 1956.

If Ike gets in I'll have to go back to the farm and plant some sweet potatoes behind the barn.

If I get too hungry I'll steal roasting ears, and try to get by for the next 4 years.

(Author(s) Unknown)

One day of praying
Seven days of fun
Your chance of going to Heaven
Is six to one.

Chorus I
20 cents cotton
40 cents meat
How in the world,
Can a poor man eat?

Chorus II
I killed a shoat.
I took it to town.
I sold the shoat for 20 cents a pound.

Chorus III
The very next week,
I had to buy it back,
For 80 cents a pound
In a paper sack.

REPEAT: Chorus I

The Bonus Man

(This poem was taught in 1935 to my brother Aaron Jr. It was taught by the one-room schoolhouse instructor, Mrs. Lucy Hall)

1

A V-8 Ford I had longed to gain
And then along my bonus came.
I bought the Ford and I hit the road
To show my friends my V-8 Ford.

2

I should have bought a home instead
To care for me when I am old and almost dead.
But government bonds, and V-8 Fords have
Caused the Bonus Man to plan for a better life and load.

3

He plans by night. He plans by day,
What girl he'll jilt the coming day.
Then after all the money is spent,
He roams around, all broke and bent.

4

With not a cent to pay his rent
Then the V-8 Ford goes back to Kent.
So take a tip from me about his fall
Buy yourself a home, and let the V-8 Ford stall.

"The School Train"

Author Unknown
Excerpts from one Teacher's Instructor magazine

(How it is now a day – 1958, and so on)

You don't run the engine.
You can't even ring the bell
But just let the darn thing jump the track,
And see who catches hell.   (Teachers!)

"This Time"

The folks getting mighty smart,
In every kind of way.
Somebody done got so smart,
and changed the time of day.

SOAP OPERA BLUES

She left me sitting on the **Edge of Night** without a **Guiding Light**, and trying to **Search for Tomorrow**.

She learned how to drink from the **Doctors' Wives**. She learned how to cheat on **Days of Our Lives**. That's also how I lost my **Love of Life**. She said she had only **One Life to Live**. Yet, thank Heaven I will soon be in **Another World** with **All of My Children**.

A THOUGHT FOR
"THE YOUNG AND RESTLESS"

As you are, so once was I. As I am, you soon will be.

> Three things that cannot be learned in school:
> 1. Sin
> 2. Righteousness
> 3. Judgment

Morale of the Story:
"Don't try to be what you ain't because if you try to be
what you ain't, then you ain't what you is."

"Billy Pig and Fairy Foot"

By them, through Holy Hope, and Love, we feel in
our serene to be connected with the Lodge above.

"Thoughts For Today"
(Written on a Wednesday)

Joy and hope can come alive in us as we give
ourselves to Christ in devotion and obedience.

Immortal and Unseen

by Cleveland Wilkins

Now the evening sun is sinking,
Now that is all that is on my mind;
Although I'm not with my Darling,
I'll love you 'til the end of time.

November 14, 1952

CHURCH QUOTES

(Authors unknown)

- "Learn to praise God."

- Give and not to count the cost

- Toil and not seek for rest.

- Labor and not ask for any reward.

- You will live –If you die in Christ:
    - Life is short.
    - Death is sure.
    - Sin is the cause.
    - Christ is the Cure

- Five Steps to Perfect Peace
    1. Worry about no things – things in your life.
    2. Pray about every thing
    3. Be thankful for all things
    4. Think on the best things

- Take Life Like You Find It. But Don't Leave It Like It Is.

- He who will not fall down, ought not to walk in slippery places.

- The devil promises much, but pays little.

- A little flatter now and then, makes big fools of many men.

- Love can wait. Lust can't wait.

- Man got to live? No, Man got to die.

- Do the right things, and the God of peace shall be with you as you do something worthwhile.

- Ending up with what you didn't start with…

LOCAL FIRSTS

A. The First "Doctrines and Discipline of the Colored Methodist Episcopal Church in America was published by W.H. Miles in 1881, Louisville, Kentucky; then reprinted in 1883 by E. Cottress, of Byhalia, Mississippi; Then reprinted in 1970 by The Christian Methodist Episcopal Church Publishing House in Memphis, Tennessee, M.C. Pettigrew, publishing agent

B. Rev. A.V. Warren Sr., first sermon after Annual Conference, October 10, 1982. "He Opened the Book" Rev. Warren's first sermon in the new year of 1984: You Got to Move (analogy – "Abram get thee out of the land." Satan was kicked out of Heaven.)

C. First Black Sheriff of Marshall County killed, May 7, 1986; Mr. Osborne Bell (born July 14, 1935), a former teacher at Humphrey Elementary and Sims High School, was the first black elected sheriff in Mississippi since Reconstruction. He served as sheriff from 1980-1986. His campaign was in 1979. He was a vice president for the J.F. Brittenum & Son Funeral Home, and a Korean War veteran. His talent included being lead singer and co-founder of the Friendly Travelers Gospel Quartet.

D. Bainesville Elementary is known to have been built in 1945. It burned in 1967. During 1945, school only lasted five months.

E.   Ida Baker Wells Barnett, a Holly Springs, Mississippi native, was a strong activist against the lynching of Blacks in the South.

She founded the Negro Fellowship League in 1908, becoming its first president. She was among the blacks to form the NAACP (National Association for the Advancement of Colored People). She married Ferdinand L. Barnett, a journalist who helped write the World's Fair booklet. A museum is presently named in her honor, at the corner of Highway #7 in Holly Springs, Mississippi.

F. In 1975 Mississippi's school officials were still allowed to use severe corporal punishment. One discipline notice read "choice - three days or five licks".

G. The first graduate of Rust College was Mary Ford-Holiday, a native of Okolona, Mississippi. She graduated May 17, 1917.

H. Eddie Lee Smith was the first Black Mayor of Marshall County.

I.   Lawrence H. Autry was the first black superintendent of Marshall County.

J. Three (3) Fishes and 5 Loaves of Bread" was Rev. Buchanan's last sermon, Sunday August 13, 1978.

School Days Folk Sayings

(Author Unknown)

ROPE-JUMPING RHYME
One, two, 3, 4, 5, 6, 7.
All good children go to Heaven.
When they get there, the Angels will say,
Henry Jr. High children, right this way.

Mrs. Coleman was a teacher at Henry Jr. High School, though she
is not the originator of the rhyme.

"Our Fear of Machines"

(An essay)

Author Unknown

1. Man fears machines because of jobs. One machine can replace ten men or more. Machines cause man to be lonely, because there is no one to communicate with on his job. Machine is drawing man away from church, because of radios and television

2. Without machine man would not be able to farm as much. He couldn't travel as far and as fast. Machines help in communication, building, fixing bad roads, and are life-saving in hospitals.

3. No and yes, for this reason- some people are born with a certain talent where others must be trained. They may not be able to use the machines.

4. Machines may A) take away man's job. B) Make him lonely. C) Without the know-how, machines can be dangerous.

5. Finally mankind, love one another. Machines cannot love.

Me
My Sister's
and Mama's
Cooking
Shorts

by Florence Virginia Wilkins Coleman
and
Della Bernice Wilkins Wadsworth Phillips

(Disclaimer: Recipes not recommended for dieters)

M.O.R.E. Publishers Corp.   St. Louis, MO

Foreword

A cookbook must be developed, tried, and tasted without conversation. So I have included a little bit of dialogue, short stories, anecdotes and memory items that with tickle your ticklebone while you use the delicious recipes inside. Enjoy from the halls of Mississippi Southern Belles' homes.

Butter Roll Dessert

Della Wadsworth Phillips

First you must already know how to make dough for biscuits.

Ingredients

3 eggs beaten well (optional) [Note: I don't use eggs myself. Others have tried it this way. The sauce may be lumpy if you do.]
½ gallon of milk
1 tablespoon Vanilla Extract
½ teaspoon nutmeg
1- 2-½ cup of sugar
Sweeten to your taste.
½ cup Pet milk
Kneaded biscuit dough
1 stick of butter or margarine

Steps

Using self-rising flour, make up dough.
Take kneaded dough and roll thin into a large square shape.
With a sharp wet knife, cut the square into 2-8 equal sections.
On each square, sprinkle some of the sugar and nutmeg lightly. Place at least three 1/8-inch squares of butter on each strip. Fold each piece into long, roll-like shape. Crease the sides so that the dough will remain closed during cooking.
Grease a wide loaf pan or glass baking dish with butter. This helps the dough to brown under the bottom and avoid unwanted sticky dough. Grease each roll top with soft butter.

Now mix the rest of the sugar, nutmeg, vanilla extract, and milk in a large mixing bowl. Stir well.

Pour some of the mixture over the folded dough strips. Use just enough to cover all of the strips, but not enough to boil over in the oven during cooking.

Place the pan into the 400 degrees oven. Turn the oven down to 350 and let cook for approximately 45 minutes, or until the rolls' crust tops are golden brown.

Enjoy.

Now with the rest of the mixture, combine with the well-beaten eggs that you did not put into the butter roll. Make homemade, vanilla ice cream. Boil the mixture for about five (5) minutes. You must continue to stir while it is boiling. If you do not stir, the mixture will easily scorch and burn. When the mixture thickens into a custard-like substance, remove and cool.

Pour into individual, decorated freezer dishes or a large pan. Let custard freeze.

If you have an ice cream mixer, this will create more fun.

Quick, No-Bake Banana Pudding:

For One Person

Ingredients

Small glass baking dish
1 box of vanilla wafers
4 bananas
1 cup of milk
¼ cup of sugar
Marshmallows or Whipped Cream (or other topping that you desire)

Steps

A. Line the bottom of the glass pan with vanilla wafers (as many as you desire).
B. Slice two of the bananas as a layer on top of the vanilla wafers.
C. Place another layer of vanilla wafers on top of the bananas. Add the fourth banana if desired.
D. Set aside until you prepare the other ingredients.
E. Boil the cup of milk. Stir constantly.
F. Add your own teaspoon full of flavor such as vanilla, banana, lemon, or coconut.
G. Sweeten with the recommended amount of sugar or sweeten to your taste.
H. Pour boiling milk over both layers of bananas and cookies.
I. Let cool and eat with your own topping variety.

From Florence

Tips:

Get good and ripe, clean bananas!

Pyrex pans are my favorite for cooking.

To preserve the bananas, cover them with a paper towel, place them in the produce section of the refrigerator, and they will last longer.

No one can eat a whole bunch at one time. Being out in the fruit bowl on the table makes them look pretty. However, heat makes them ripen too quickly.

Once you take them out of the refrigerator, let them sit at room temperature and warm. Eat quickly.

Old-Fashioned Rolls

By Charlene Wilkins Bunch (Niece)

Ingredients

¼ cup of shortening

2 eggs

2 packages of dry yeast

2-3 tablespoon sugar

1 ½ cup of warm water

½ cup of honey

1 1/3 teaspoon of salt

5 ½ cups of flour

1 rolling pin

1 cup, preferably without handles

Steps

In a small mixing bowl, stir water, the yeast, and the 3 tablespoons of sugar.

Then in a larger bowl, first beat the eggs (whole). Combine the eggs, honey, salt, shortening and yeast mixture.

Slowly add flour with the mixture. Let that sit aside. Grease another bowl and now place the bread mixture in the greased bowl. Cover it with a red towel or with your favorite color cloth.

Place that bowl mixture in warm area for 3 hours until the dough rises to ½ of its original size.

Spread wax paper out on the counter or table work area.

Roll out the dough with a rolling pin.

Once the dough ball is flattened, take a regular kitchen cup if you do not have a biscuit cutter, and cut out the dough into separate circles or squares.

Place each into a lightweight, baking pan, if you have one.

Let that dough rise some more.

Heat the oven 350 degrees for about 5 minutes. Now place the pan and separated rolls into the oven.

Bake until the tops are brown to your preference.

Serve hot with butter. If you must wait to eat, let rolls cool and cover with plastic wrap until the family is ready. Then remove the plastic covering and warm rolls enough to melt the butter.

Opened-Face Apple Pie
(For beginners and non-cooks)

by Angelee Coleman Grider (Daughter)

Wash and peel 4 apples (8 when you are expecting a crowd). If you like the hull, you may leave the apples unpeeled. For safety measure, wash in mild soapy water to remove the dirt chemical spray, and rinse well.

Melt 1-2 sticks of margarine in a medium sized baking pan. For those with a weak stomach, just use one stick of butter.

Combine and stir the apples and the butter in the pan. Be sure that the apples are well coated.

Add your own special flavoring of spices: cinnamon, lemon, nutmeg, vanilla extract etc. Stir well.

Combine in the pan or a large mixing bowl, the buttered, seasoned apples with one cup of flour and ½ cup of sugar. Add more flour if needed to coat the apples. Some apples are larger than others.

If you used a bowl, place the mixture back into the buttered pan. Let sit for 5 minutes while you heat the oven to 400 degrees.

Now bake until coating is light brown on top.

Serve with whipped cream, milk, ice cream, or a hot cup of tea.

Fried Pies

Della Wadsworth Phillips

Ingredients

Dough
Favorite fruit cooked
Soft butter
Vanilla extract
Your favorite seasoning such as nutmeg, cinnamon, lemon, etc.

What do you do next?
Prepare the fruit as if you were going to can preserves. Peel and cook well. Pies work well with apples, peaches, or pears.
Mash the fruit until there are no lumps left.
Roll the dough thin with a rolling pin.
Cut dough into triangular shapes.
Spread fruit mixture on top of each piece of dough triangle. Fold. Crimp the edges closed. Place on a butter greased baking sheet or in a long pan.
Spread the top of the bread with butter. Sprinkle with your favorite spice to enhance the flavor of the fruit.
Place in the oven. Bake in a 350 degree oven for approximately 4-5 minutes or until the crusts are brown.
Remove from oven and cool on a cooling rack.
You may reduce the use of butter if you prefer.

Old Fashioned Fish Fry

Tips: Only buy fresh fish. If feeding children, cook the boneless style. Batter the fish to your taste of seasoning. Cornbread, salt, and pepper are your basic ingredients.

Use an old-fashioned kettle pot, outside. Heat grease to medium boiling. A hot boil will cause the crust of the fish to brown before the meat is done. Then cooking longer will only cause the fish to burn and turn black.

Carefully dip each piece into the hot oil. Once the crust is brown, remove the fish from the oil. To assure that the meat is well cooked, place inside of a hot oven for about 15 minutes before eating, or microwave for about 2 minutes.

Preparation Secrets

Greens: Buy the fresh-looking ones. Wash the greens well in cold water. Be sure the sand and dirt are all out of the leafy green crevices. Boil the small piece of hog jowl for 40 minutes before adding the greens to the hot water. Cook until tender.

Biscuits: Grease the bottom of the glass ovenware pan before placing the biscuits inside. When the tops are brown, lightly grease with your favorite butter. Place a top over the biscuits and they will stay soft.

Place leftover biscuits in plastic zipped bags, or leave in the covered pan. Place in the refrigerator.

Chicken: It is good that there is now clean, organic chickens being raised. Yet some of us still want the chemical-induced ones, so before you cook the chicken, let's eliminate some of the blood.

www.ingramcontent.com/pod-product-compliance
Lightning Source LLC
Chambersburg PA
CBHW071209130626
46555CB00004B/1643